NEW MEXICO

in words and pictures

BY DENNIS B. FRADIN

MAPS BY LEN W. MEENTS

Consultant
Dr. Donald C. Cutter
Professor of Southwestern History
The University of New Mexico

CHILDRENS PRESS, CHICAGO

For my parents,
Myron and Selma Fradin

For their help, the author thanks:

Dr. Barry S. Kues, Department of Geology, University of New Mexico
Stewart Peckham, Assistant Director of the Anthropology Bureau,
Museum of New Mexico
Jodi Cohen, New Mexico State Office of Indian Affairs
Thomas E. Chavez, Curator of Collections, History Bureau, Museum
of New Mexico
Orlando Romero, Southwest Librarian, New Mexico State Library

Elephant Butte

Library of Congress Cataloging in Publication Data

Fradin, Dennis B
  New Mexico in words and pictures.

  SUMMARY: Presents the history, cities, Indians,
animal life, tourist sights, industries, and
famous citizens of this state where the first
atomic bomb was made and exploded.
  1. New Mexico—Juvenile literature. [1. New
Mexico] II. Meents, Len W. III. Title.
F796.3.F7   978.9   81-298
ISBN 0-516-03931-8   AACRI

Picture Acknowledgments:
TOM WINTER—cover, 2, 6 (2), 15 (left), 17, 18 (left top & bottom, bott
  right), 21 (right), 23 (right), 25 (3), 26, 27, 29 (2), 31 (4), 32 (2), 37,
MUSEUM OF NEW MEXICO—9 (right), 12, 13 (2), 23 (left top & botto
  41 (2)
COMMERCE & INDUSTRY DEPARTMENT, TOURISM & TRAVEL
  DIVISION, SANTA FE—15 (right), 24 (2), 28, 33, 36
LAS CRUCES CONVENTION & VISITORS BUREAU—16 (2)
DEPARTMENT OF DEVELOPMENT, STATE OF NEW MEXICO—22
DEPARTMENT OF ENERGY, ALBUQUERQUE—21 (right)
AMERICAN AIRLINES—21 (left)
U.S. DEPARTMENT OF THE INTERIOR, NATIONAL PARK SERVICE—
  WHITE SANDS NATIONAL MONUMENT, 34 (2);
  EL MORRO NATIONAL MONUMENT, 18 (top right)
NPS, SOUTHWEST REGION, FRED MANG, JR. PHOTOGRAPHER—9
  (left), 35

  COVER PICTURE—Black Mesa near Santa Fe

New Mexico

New Mexico (NOO MEX • ih • koh) is a lovely state in the southwestern United States. It has deserts and forests. It has mountains and plains.

New Mexico is a top mining state. Oil, natural gas, copper, and coal are some of its mining products. New Mexico has a lot of cattle and sheep, too.

New Mexico is also rich in Indian history. It has buildings and towns made hundreds of years ago by Indians. Over 100,000 Indians live in the state today.

Do you know where our country's oldest road is located? Or where you can see the Carlsbad (CARLZ • bad) Caverns? Do you know where the first atomic bomb was blasted? Or where Billy the Kid became a famous outlaw? You'll soon see that the answer to all these questions is: New Mexico, the Land of Enchantment!

Long before there were people in New Mexico, dinosaurs lived there. Camarasaurus (cam • ah • rah • SORE • us) was there. He ate plants. Tyrannosaurs (ty • RAN • ah • SORES) were there, too. They ate other dinosaurs. Camels, huge birds, and crocodiles (CROCK • uh • diles) also lived in New Mexico. So did mastodons (MASS • tah • donz). They looked like big, furry elephants. Fossils (FAWSS • ills) of these animals have been found.

The state is a great place to hunt for fossils. In 1956 a nine-year-old boy found fossil mastodon teeth.

New Mexico is also a fine place to hunt for remains of ancient peoples. Many groups of early people lived there.

People first came to New Mexico over 12,000 years ago. The early people hunted with stone-tipped spears.

Folsom (FOHL • sum) Man lived in New Mexico at least 10,000 years ago. Folsom Man made spearheads known as *Folsom points*. A black cowboy, George McJunkin, first found evidence of Folsom Man near Folsom, New Mexico.

By 2,000 years ago the Anasazi (an • ah • SAH • zee) Indians were living in New Mexico. They began to farm and build villages. One group of Anasazi, the Basketmakers, made baskets out of grasses and other plants. A later Anasazi group, the Cliff Dwellers, built stone houses high up in the cliffs.

Taos Pueblo

By 400 years ago the Anasazi were building houses that were two to three stories tall. These houses, which look like big apartment buildings, are called *pueblos* (PWEB • lohz). And the Indians who built them are now called Pueblo Indians.

Spaniards were the first non-Indians in New Mexico. By the mid-1500s Spain ruled Mexico. The Spanish wanted gold. Stories were told of golden cities to the north. These cities were called the *Seven Cities of Cibola* (SEE • boh • lah).

6

In 1539 the Spanish priest Marcos de Niza (MAR •
kohss theh NEE • zah) came to New Mexico. He claimed
the area for Spain. He also claimed to have seen the
golden cities from far away. It is thought that he really
saw a Pueblo Indian village that looked golden in the
sunset. From 1540 to 1542 the Spaniard Coronado (kor •
ah • NAH • doh) looked for the golden cities in New
Mexico. He never found them. But he did explore many
places in what is now the southwestern United States.

By 1581 Spaniards were traveling between Mexico and
New Mexico on a road called *El Camino Real* (el cah •
MEE • noh ray • AHL), meaning *The Royal Road*. This is
now the oldest road in the United States.

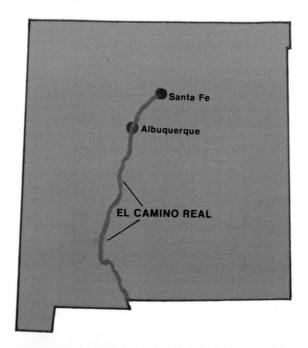

The Spaniard Antonio de Espejo (an • TONE • ee • oh day ess • PAY • ho) explored New Mexico from 1582 to 1583. Espejo reported that the area had great mineral wealth. He said that it was good for grazing cattle. He also said that the land might be good for farming. He must have had a crystal ball! Mineral wealth, ranching, and farming are important to New Mexico today.

In 1598 the Spanish built their first colony in what they called *Nuevo Mexico* (NWAY • voh MEH • hee • koh) — New Mexico. This colony was named San Juan de Los Caballeros (san HWAN day loss cah • bahl • YEROS). It was founded by Juan de Oñate (HWAN de oh • NYAH • tay). You can see where Oñate wrote his name on a big rock called Inscription Rock.

In 1610 the Spanish founded Santa Fe (SAN • tah FAY). That year Santa Fe became the capital of the Spanish province of New Mexico.

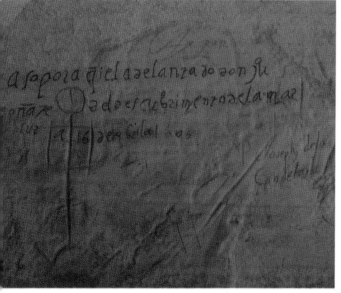

Above: Quaria State Monument, near Mountainair. Quaria was built in 1620 by Spanish missionaries with the help of Indian labor. This church and the small village that once stood here were abandoned in 1675 due to drought, famine, and constant Indian raids.
Left: Inscription Rock, El Morro National Monument

Spanish priests came to New Mexico. Their job was to teach the Indians about Christianity. Churches called *missions* were built. But the Indians did not want to give up their own religion. And they did not like it when the Spanish treated them poorly. In one big fight, in 1680, a Pueblo Indian named Popé (POPE • ay) led a revolt. The Indians drove the Spanish out of New Mexico for about twelve years. But then in 1692 the Spanish took over again and ruled until 1821. During this time only a few thousand Spanish people went to live there.

In 1821 Mexico freed itself from Spain. Mexico now ruled New Mexico. Not for very long, though!

American fur trappers and traders had entered New Mexico in the early 1800s. Then in 1822 William Becknell, an American, brought some wagons from Missouri to Santa Fe. The trail he opened became known as the Santa Fe Trail. Many American traders went to Santa Fe on this trail. They brought goods from the east to Santa Fe. They traded those goods for furs, silver, and mules.

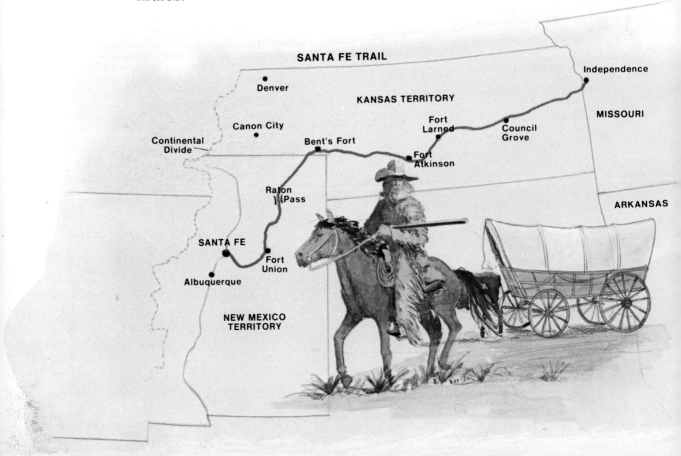

During the 1800s Americans were moving farther and farther west. As they did this the United States government took control of lands in the west. From 1846 to 1848 the United States and Mexico fought over land. The United States won this fight, which is called the Mexican War. The United States then took over a large area which included much of New Mexico.

New Mexico wasn't a state yet. In 1850 it became a territory. This meant it was ruled by the United States. At this time the Territory of New Mexico included most of Arizona and parts of Utah, Nevada, and Colorado. But by 1863, New Mexico had the borders it has today.

Americans came to New Mexico to hunt for gold, silver, and other metals. Some came to ranch. New Mexico now had three main groups living there, as it has today. There were the Indians, who had been there first. There were the people of Spanish background. And there were the English-speaking people who had come from other parts of the United States. By 1870, over 90,000 people lived in New Mexico.

Lincoln County Courthouse is now a museum. Billy the Kid killed two deputies during his daring escape from here in 1881. Two months later Billy was shot by the town's sheriff, Pat Garrett.

New Mexico was the scene of much fighting in the second half of the 19th century. The Civil War was fought from 1861 to 1865 between the Northern and Southern states. During this war, the South took control of much of New Mexico. But the North won it back.

Then from 1876 to 1881 New Mexico had a war of its own. It was called the "Lincoln County War." It was fought between two groups of settlers. Some think that the fight started because of cattle stealing. A number of men were killed and wounded. The outlaw Billy the Kid took part in the fighting.

Left: Geronimo, Chiricahua Apache. This 1884
photo was taken by A. Frank Randall.
Above: Remains of the troop barracks at
Fort Selden State Monument. Fort
Selden was built in 1865 along the Rio
Grande to protect settlers from Apache raids.

New Mexico was a dangerous place during these
years. There were range wars and gunfights, cattle
rustlings and hangings. Even inside the dance halls there
were signs that said "Don't Shoot The Musicians. They
Are Doing The Best They Can."

In still more fighting, the Apache (ah • PATCH • ee)
chief, Geronimo (jer • RON • ih • moh), led Indians on raids
on white settlements in Arizona and New Mexico.
Geronimo was one of the last Indians to fight the
government. The fighting ended when Geronimo
surrendered in 1886.

13

Railroads came to New Mexico in the late 1800s. More farmers arrived by train. More miners came also. Cattle were sent to markets in the east by train. Copper and other mining products were sent out, too. By 1900 over 195,000 people lived in New Mexico.

For years, New Mexicans had wanted their territory to become a state. Finally, on January 6, 1912, New Mexico became our 47th state. Santa Fe was the capital. Over the years, New Mexico was given many nicknames. It was called the *Sunshine State* because of its clear, sunny weather. It was called the *Cactus State* because of the cactus plants that grow in its desert areas. It was called the *Land of Enchantment* because of its beauty and interesting history. The *Land of Enchantment* is now the state's main nickname.

Trail riders explore the Pecos Wilderness.
The Sangre de Cristo Mountains are in the
background.
Left: Santa Rita Copper Mine

Do you remember how Coronado and other Spaniards had looked for gold in New Mexico? In 1922 a treasure was found in the state. This was oil. Oil became New Mexico's main mining product. Natural gas, copper, and uranium are also found in New Mexico today. The Land of Enchantment is one of our top mining states.

Ranching and farming are big in the state, too. New Mexico is a leader for raising sheep.

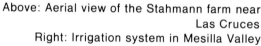
Above: Aerial view of the Stahmann farm near
Las Cruces
Right: Irrigation system in Mesilla Valley

When it came to growing crops, however, New Mexico
farmers had a problem. There wasn't enough rainfall.
Dams have helped to solve this problem. The dams hold
back water that is sent to farms when it is needed. Many
wells have been dug so that underground water can also
be used. Bringing water to dry farmland is called
irrigation (ear • rah • GAY • shun). Thanks to irrigation,
New Mexico farmers now grow many crops.

16

Los Alamos began as a "secret town" during World War II.

During World War I (1914-1918) and World War II (1939-1945) New Mexico's sheep and cattle ranches provided our country's soldiers with food and clothes. Its metals were used to make ships and airplanes.

A big event in world history took place in New Mexico during World War II. The U.S. government built a secret town, Los Alamos (los AL • ah • mos), in the state. The first atom bomb was made there. It was tested at the Trinity (TRIN • ih • tee) Site. The atom bombs dropped on Japan in 1945 were made in Los Alamos, too. These bombs ended World War II. Research for making atomic weapons is done in New Mexico today. Work is also done on the peaceful uses of nuclear energy.

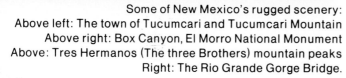

Some of New Mexico's rugged scenery:
Above left: The town of Tucumcari and Tucumcari Mountain
Above right: Box Canyon, El Morro National Monument
Above: Tres Hermanos (The three Brothers) mountain peaks
Right: The Rio Grande Gorge Bridge.

You have learned about some of New Mexico's history. Now it is time for a trip—in words and pictures— through the Land of Enchantment.

New Mexico is the fifth biggest of our 50 states. Except for its southern border, which looks like a flight of steps, New Mexico is square-shaped. Colorado is New Mexico's neighbor state to the north. Oklahoma and Texas are to the east. Texas and Mexico are to the south. Arizona is to the west. Utah touches New Mexico's northwest corner.

Pretend you're in a jet high above New Mexico. Below, the state is a wonderland of color. Do you see all the mountain ranges? The Sangre de Cristo (SANG • gray deh KRIS • toh), Sacramento (sack • rah • MEN • toh), and Zuni (ZOO • nee) are three of them. You can see rivers, such as the Rio Grande (REE • oh GRAN • day) and the Pecos (PAY • kohss). You can see deserts and forests.

Your airplane is landing in Albuquerque (AL • buh • ker kee). The city was founded in 1706 by Francisco Cuervo y Valdes (fran • SISS • koh KWARE • voh ee val • DEZ). He was governor of New Mexico when it was a Spanish province. Today, Albuquerque is the state's biggest city.

Visit Albuquerque's Old Town. This is the old part of the city. You'll see the Church of San Felipe de Neri (san feh • LEE • pay day NAIR • ee) in the Old Town. This church was built way back in 1706.

Today, Albuquerque is a center for atomic research. At the Sandia (san • DEE • ah) Laboratories, research is done to develop nuclear weapons. Work is also done to find new energy sources. At Albuquerque's National Atomic Museum you can learn about nuclear energy.

Many kinds of people live in Albuquerque. You'll see Indians and Spanish Americans. You'll meet people of many other backgrounds. The people of Albuquerque work at many jobs. Some make clothes. Others make foods. Computers and adobe houses are also made in the area.

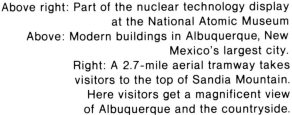

Above right: Part of the nuclear technology display at the National Atomic Museum
Above: Modern buildings in Albuquerque, New Mexico's largest city.
Right: A 2.7-mile aerial tramway takes visitors to the top of Sandia Mountain. Here visitors get a magnificent view of Albuquerque and the countryside.

Albuquerque is also a center for education. The University of New Mexico is there. Here students study law, medicine, science, and many other subjects. The University of Albuquerque and Southwestern Indian Polytechnic Institute are also in the city.

State Capitol

Santa Fe is northeast of Albuquerque. Santa Fe has been the capital of New Mexico since 1610. It is the oldest of all the capital cities in America.

Visit the State Capitol building. This is where lawmakers from all across New Mexico meet. You can watch them as they make laws for their state.

Because Santa Fe is New Mexico's capital, many of the city's people work for the state government. Others work for United States agencies located in the city.

You'll enjoy the Palace of the Governors in Santa Fe. Built by the Spanish in 1610, it is one of the oldest public buildings in America. Spanish governors once ruled from this building. Pueblo Indians attacked the palace in the revolt of 1680. Today, the Palace of the Governors is a museum where you can learn about New Mexico history.

The Palace of the Governors (top left), built in 1610, is now a history museum. In August it is the site of the annual Indian market (left). Indians sell pottery, leather goods, jewelry, and other crafts from temporary booths. Above: The Santa Fe Opera House is a beautiful outdoor theater.

Santa Fe has some fine museums. At the branches of the Museum of New Mexico in Santa Fe you can learn about art, New Mexico history, and the Indian people.

The Mission of San Miguel (SAN mee • GHEL) was built in the 1600s. It is one of the oldest churches in the United States.

Many of Santa Fe's buildings are made of adobe (ah • DOE • bee)—sun-baked bricks. Because of Santa Fe's interesting buildings and history, many artists and writers make their homes in the city.

Above: Deer dancers perform at the Gallup
Inter-Tribal ceremonial.
Right: Ruins of Tyvonye, a big community house
in Frijoles Canyon, located in Bandelier
National Monument near Santa Fe

Visit Bandelier (band • del • EER) National Monument near Santa Fe. Ancient Indian cliff dwellings can be seen there. The Puyé Cliff Dwellings, also near Santa Fe, look like apartment buildings. They were built about 600 years ago by Indians. At Chaco (CHAH • koh) Canyon National Monument, Aztec (AZ • teck) Ruins National Monument, and other places in the state, you can see ruins of old Indian communities.

You'll enjoy exploring such ruins. They remind you that Indians have lived in New Mexico for thousands of years. While in New Mexico, you may come across pottery pieces made by Indians of long ago. Scientists are still digging to learn more about the early people of New Mexico.

Traditional Indian dances and a rodeo are some of the crowd-pleasing events at the annual Inter-Tribal Indian Ceremonial in Gallup.

Today, over 100,000 Indians live in New Mexico. Most live on lands reserved for Indians. Such lands are called *reservations.* Other Indians live in cities and towns throughout the state.

The Navajo (NAH • vah • ho) are the biggest tribe in New Mexico. A huge Navajo reservation lies in northwestern New Mexico and extends into three other states. The Pueblo Indians are second in number in New Mexico. There are 19 Pueblo Indian villages in the state. The Apache are New Mexico's third largest Indian group.

Indians work at just about every kind of job. There are Indian teachers, doctors, and lawyers. There are Indian cattle ranchers and construction workers. There are Indian businessmen. There are also tribally-owned businesses. The Navajo and Pueblo Indians have their own cattle businesses. The Navajo have wool and weaving businesses. The Apaches are in the oil and natural gas businesses.

New Mexico Indians have kept their own culture alive. Indian children are taught their native language. Parents and grandparents teach children the history of their people. The Indians have also maintained old ceremonies and dances.

An Indian woman weaves a traditional design.

Ship Rock

Many Indians have kept the ancient crafts. The Pueblo Indians are famed for making pottery and baskets. The Navajo are famous for weaving blankets.

The Indians have many stories about the land. According to one story, the Navajo people were once losing a battle in another place. The Navajo prayed to be saved. Suddenly the ground they were on rose high into the sky. It turned into a ship and took them to northwestern New Mexico where they still live. The hill that looks like a ship is called Ship Rock. You can see it on the Navajo Indian Reservation.

New Mexico also has a large population of Spanish-American people. The state has many towns and cities with Spanish names. Española (es • pan • NYOH • la), El Rito (el REE • toh), Velarde (vel • AR • day), Hernandez (her • NAN • dez), and Socorro (so • KOR • ah) are just five of them. Spanish-American holidays and festivals are popular too. You'll see signs in New Mexico printed in both Spanish and English.

Four Corners Monument is at the far northwestern corner of New Mexico. This is the only place in America where four states meet. The states are New Mexico, Arizona, Utah, and Colorado. You can stand in all four states at once!

Four Corners Monument

Above: Silver City, Gateway to the Gila Wilderness
Left: Trout streams and canyons are found
throughout the western wilderness.

Farmington is the biggest city in northwestern New Mexico. Coal is mined in the Farmington area. Oil and natural gas are also produced in the area.

From Farmington, take a trip down the western side of New Mexico. You can go for many miles without seeing a town. You remember that New Mexico is one of our largest states. But it is low on the list in number of people. There are only about nine people for every square mile in New Mexico. Many parts of the state have been saved as wilderness areas where no cars are permitted.

Down in southwestern New Mexico you will enter Gila (HEE • lah) National Forest. In all, about a quarter of the state is wooded. Cottonwoods, aspens, spruce, ponderosa pine, and piñons (PIN • yuns) are just some of the kinds of trees you'll see. The piñon or nut pine is the New Mexico state tree.

You can see many animals of the forests, mountains and plains in New Mexico. You can see mule deer and whitetail deer. You can spot black bears. Coyotes live in New Mexico. Farmers don't like them because they kill sheep. Mountain lions can be found. They hunt deer and porcupines. Pronghorn antelopes live on the grasslands. Foxes, bobcats, and prairie dogs are some of the state's other animals.

As you travel on New Mexico's roads, you may see a funny-looking bird that spends much of its time running. This bird is called the roadrunner. The roadrunner eats mice and snakes. The roadrunner is the state bird of New Mexico.

Animals that live in New Mexico include the kit fox
(below left), diamondback rattlesnake (above left),
prairie dog (above center), and the mule deer (above right).

The deserts also have a wealth of animal life. There
isn't very much water on a desert. The kangaroo rat—
which can jump like a kangaroo—doesn't drink any
water. It gets water from the food it eats. Gila monsters
live in the deserts. They are big, poisonous lizards. You'll
also find tarantulas (tah • RAN • chu • laz) in the deserts.
These spiders aren't very pretty—but they aren't
very harmful, either. New Mexico's black widow spiders,
however, *are* poisonous.

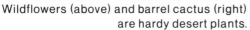
Wildflowers (above) and barrel cactus (right)
are hardy desert plants.

The deserts have their own kinds of plant life, too.
You'll see cactus plants. They can go without water for
long periods of time. You'll also see yucca plants. The
Indians made a drink from the fruit of the yucca plant.
They made soap from the stems and roots. The yucca
flower, which is shaped like a bell, is the New Mexico
state flower.

Head down to Las Cruces (las KROO • sess) in southern
New Mexico. The city lies on the Rio Grande. Las Cruces
(meaning *the crosses*) was founded in 1849. Today, New

Mexico State University is in Las Cruces. Students there study business and science. They study education and farming. Las Cruces is in the middle of a big farming area.

There are "ghost towns" near Las Cruces—and in other areas of the state. Long ago, people built these towns as they searched for gold and other treasures. When the metals were mined out, the people left. But the buildings in the towns still stand. Mogollon (moe • GO • yone), Lake Valley, Kingston, and Madrid (mah • DRID) are just four New Mexico ghost towns.

Mogollon is a ghost town off U.S. Highway 180 in southwestern New Mexico. Following a gold strike in the early 1870s, the town's population once reached 2,000. Today it is deserted.

White Sands National Monument

Visit White Sands National Monument, not far from Las Cruces. The gypsum (JIP • sum) sand there is as white as snow. You'll enjoy sliding down the sand banks and dunes. Nearby is the White Sands Missile Range. The U.S. government tests missiles and rockets there.

Head to Carlsbad Caverns National Park in southeastern New Mexico. Carlsbad Cavern is the main cave in the park. It took millions of years for water to eat away at the rock and form Carlsbad Cavern and the other caves in the park. You'll enjoy a tour of Carlsbad Cavern. One part of Carlsbad Cavern, the Big Room, is 4000 feet long. That means that over 13 football fields

Rock formations, Carlsbad Cavern

could fit inside! At night, thousands of bats fly out of the cavern entrance. Jim White, a cowboy, discovered the cavern in 1901 when he saw bats coming out of the entrance. White wasn't the first person in Carlsbad Cavern, though. Picture writings on the wall prove that Indians once lived there.

After seeing Carlsbad Caverns National Park, head out into the sunlight. You'll see many oil wells in southeastern New Mexico—and in others parts of the state. New Mexico is one of our leading states for producing oil. New Mexico is also a leader for producing natural gas.

Aztec Refinery of the El Paso Gas Company

Oil and natural gas are New Mexico's main mining products. But there are many others. New Mexico is *the* top state for mining potash. Potash is used to make fertilizer. New Mexico is a top state for mining copper. Copper is used to make pennies, wire, and many other items. New Mexico is also a top state for producing uranium. Uranium is used to make atomic bombs. It is also used to run nuclear reactors. Salt, silver, coal, and zinc are just four other New Mexico mining products. All these products help make New Mexico one of our top mining states.

Visit the city of Roswell (ROZ • well) in southeastern New Mexico. A gambler named Van C. Smith helped found Roswell in 1869. Go to the Roswell Museum and Art Gallery. You can learn about rocket ships there. You can also see paintings and sculpture there.

Roswell is in a big cattle-raising area. You'll see cattle ranches in many places in New Mexico. You'll also see sheep ranches. Cowboys watch over the cattle and sheep. Some cowboys still work on horseback. But some ride in pickup trucks or even airplanes as they watch the herds.

Cattle are raised in many parts of the state.

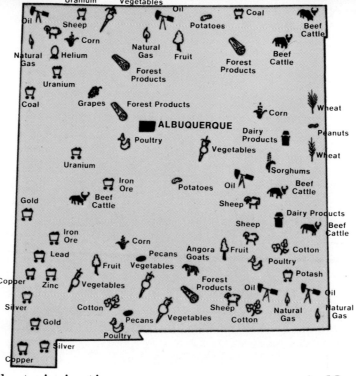

Thanks to irrigation, many crops are grown in New Mexico. Wheat, grain sorghum, alfalfa, corn, cotton, apples, chili peppers, and sugar beets are some of the state's crops.

Finish your trip at the city of Clovis (KLOH • viss), in the far eastern part of New Mexico. Clovis is nicknamed "The Cattle Capital of the Southwest" because of all the beef cattle raised in the area. A rodeo is held in Clovis every summer.

Cities, mines, and ranches can't tell New Mexico's whole story. Many interesting people have lived in the Land of Enchantment.

John Chisum (1824-1884) was born in Tennessee. He became a cattle rancher in New Mexico. It is thought that at one time he had the largest cattle herd in the world. He was called the "cow king of New Mexico." Some people think that John Chisum hired Billy the Kid as a gunman during the Lincoln County War.

William H. Bonney (1859-1881) was born in New York City. His family came to live in Silver City, New Mexico. As a boy, Bonney spent his time gambling. He was said to have killed a man when he was about 12 years old. During the Lincoln County War, a friend of Bonney's was killed. After that, Bonney used his gun to get revenge. In all, he was said to have gunned down over 20 men in his lifetime. Bonney was one of the most famous outlaws of all time. You probably have heard of him by his nickname—"Billy the Kid."

Pat Garrett (1850-1908) was born in Alabama. He became sheriff of Lincoln County, New Mexico during the Lincoln County War. In 1880 Garrett caught Billy the Kid. The Kid was sentenced to be hanged. But he escaped from jail. Two months later Pat Garrett trailed Billy the Kid to his hideout. Pat Garrett became famous as the man who shot and killed Billy the Kid.

Elizabeth Garrett (1885?-1947) was Pat Garrett's daughter. She was blind, but she loved music. She also loved New Mexico. Elizabeth Garrett wrote a song called "O, Fair New Mexico." It is one of the New Mexico state songs.

Dennis Chavez (1888-1962) was born in Los Chavez, New Mexico. He was a Spanish American. Chavez served New Mexico in the United States House of Representatives and Senate for a total of 31 years. He worked for laws to help Indians and Spanish American people. He worked to improve relations between Latin American countries and the United States.

Far Left: Dennis Chavez, United States Senator

Left: Sheriff Pat Garrett caught up with and shot Billy the Kid in Fort Sumner, New Mexico two months after Billy had escaped from the Lincoln County Courthouse.

María Montoya Martínez (1887?-1980) was born at San Ildefonso (san eel • day • FON • so) Pueblo. She was a Pueblo Indian. Maria and her husband, Julián Martínez, made black pottery using some ancient Pueblo Indian designs. Their work can be seen in museums. María Montoya Martínez was the first woman to win the United States' Indian Achievement Award.

Georgia O'Keeffe was born in Wisconsin. She became an artist and moved to Taos (TOUSE), New Mexico. Georgia O'Keeffe painted pictures of New Mexico mountains, flowers, and deserts. She is one of the most famous of all modern American artists.

Bill Mauldin was born in Mountain Park, New Mexico, in 1921. Mauldin became a cartoonist. During World War II, his cartoons showed people what the life of a soldier was like. Mauldin has also done cartoons on politics. This famous cartoonist has won two Pulitzer prizes.

Conrad Hilton (1887-1979) was born in San Antonio, New Mexico. As a boy, he helped his father rent out rooms in their adobe house. Later, Conrad Hilton became one of the biggest hotel owners in the world.

Al Unser was born in Albuquerque. He became a famous auto racer. He has won the Indianapolis 500 race three times. His brother, Bobby Unser, has won the Indianapolis 500 twice.

Harrison Schmitt was born in Santa Rita. He became a geologist. That is a scientist who studies rocks. Later he became an astronaut. In 1972 Schmitt landed on the moon. He studied the moon's surface in the longest moon visit ever—75 hours. In 1976 New Mexicans elected Harrison Schmitt to the United States Senate.

The houses of Taos seem tiny next to its tall mountains.

Home to Georgia O'Keeffe ... Dennis Chavez ... Billy the Kid ... and Harrison Schmitt.

Home also to Pueblo Indians ... Spanish Americans ... and people of many other backgrounds.

A state where you can see Carlsbad Caverns ... White Sands National Monument ... and ancient Indian ruins.

A leading state for producing oil ... natural gas ... copper ... and uranium ... and a leader for raising sheep.

This is New Mexico—the Land of Enchantment!

Facts About NEW MEXICO

Area—121,666 square miles (5th biggest state)

Greatest Distance North to South—391 miles

Greatest Distance East to West—352 miles

Borders—Colorado to the north; Oklahoma and Texas to the east; Texas and Mexico to the south; Arizona to the west; Utah to the northwest

Highest Point—13,161 feet above sea level (Wheeler Peak)

Lowest Point—2,817 feet above sea level (at Red Bluff Reservoir)

Hottest Recorded Temperature—116° (at Artesia, on June 29, 1918, and also at Orogrande, on July 14, 1934)

Coldest Recorded Temperature—Minus 50° (at Gavilan, on February 1, 1951)

Statehood—Our 47th state, on January 6, 1912

Origin of Name—New Mexico was named after the city and valley of Mexico in what was once the land (or kingdom) of New Spain

Capital—Santa Fe

Counties—32

U.S. Senators—2

U.S. Representatives—2

State Senators—42

State Representatives—70

State Songs—"O, Fair New Mexico" by Elizabeth Garrett and "Asi Es Nuevo México" by Amadeo Lucero

State Motto— *Crescit eundo* (Latin, meaning "It grows as it goes")

Main Nickname—The Land of Enchantment

Other Nicknames—The Sunshine State, the Land of Sunshine, the Cactus State

State Seal—Adopted in 1913

State Flag—Adopted in 1925

State Flower—Yucca flower

State Bird—Roadrunner

State Mammal—Black bear

State Fish—Cutthroat trout

State Gem—Turquoise

State Tree—Piñon (also known as the nut pine)

State Vegetables—The pinto bean and the chile

State Colors—Red and yellow of old Spain

Some Rivers—Rio Grande, Pecos, Canadian, San Juan, Gila

Largest Lake—Elephant Butte Reservoir

Some Mountain Ranges—Mogollon, Sangre de Cristo, San Juan, Zuni, Black, Sacramento, Jemez, San Andres

Wildlife—Mule deer, whitetail deer, black bears, coyotes, mountain lions, bobcats, pronghorn antelopes, foxes, prairie dogs, beavers, badgers, rabbits, kangaroo rats, Gila monsters, rattlesnakes and other snakes, many kinds of toads and turtles, roadrunners, ducks, pheasants, wild turkeys, many other kinds of birds

Farm Products—Beef cattle, milk, sheep, hogs, wheat, grain sorghum, broomcorn, alfalfa, corn, cotton, pecans, chili peppers, sugar beets, hay, peanuts, lettuce, tomatoes, apples

Mining—Oil, natural gas, copper, potash, uranium, coal, salt, silver, zinc

Manufacturing Products—Processed foods, electric equipment, computers and other electronic equipment, lumber, glass products, jewelry, silverware, clay products

Population—1,190,000 (1977 estimate)

Largest Cities—		
Albuquerque	294,700	(all 1979 estimates)
Santa Fe	47,400	
Las Cruces	42,100	
Roswell	41,800	
Farmington	32,700	
Hobbs	32,100	
Clovis	31,800	

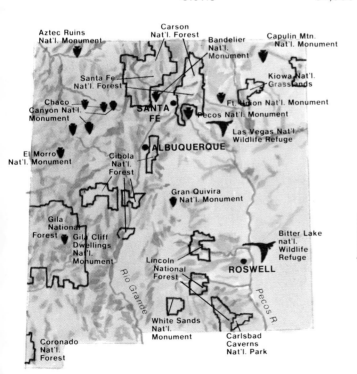

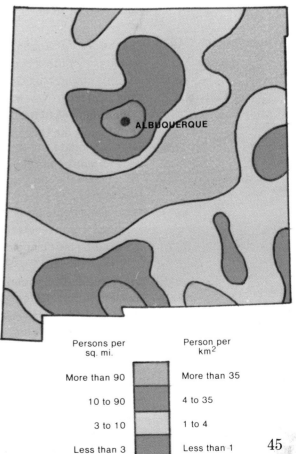

Persons per sq. mi.	Person per km²
More than 90	More than 35
10 to 90	4 to 35
3 to 10	1 to 4
Less than 3	Less than 1

45

New Mexico History

There were people in New Mexico at least 12,000 years ago; at a later time Basketmakers, Cliff Dwellers, and Pueblo Indians lived in New Mexico before explorers arrived

1539—Marcos de Niza explores New Mexico and claims it for Spain

1540-1542—The Spaniard Coronado explores New Mexico while searching for gold

1598—Juan de Oñate founds New Mexico's first Spanish settlement at San Juan de Los Caballeros

1610—Santa Fe, now the oldest capital in the United States, is founded by the Spanish

1680—Led by Popé, the Pueblo Indians drive the Spanish from New Mexico

1692—Spanish regain control of New Mexico

1706—Albuquerque is founded

1821—Mexico takes control of New Mexico

1822—William Becknell, an American, brings the first wagons from Missouri to New Mexico on the Santa Fe Trail

1834—New Mexico's first newspaper, *El Crepúsculo de la Libertad* (The Dawn of Liberty), is published in Santa Fe

1846—During the Mexican War, United States forces take control of New Mexico

1848—By the Treaty of Guadalupe Hidalgo, which ends the Mexican War, the United States gains control of New Mexico

1850—Territory of New Mexico is created by U.S. government

1853—Land is added to New Mexico by the Gadsden Purchase

1861—At the beginning of the Civil War Confederate troops take over much of New Mexico; the Union wins it back the next year

1862—Battle of Glorieta, known as the "Gettysburg of the West," was one of the turning points of the Civil War

1863—The "Long Walk," the relocation of the Navaho Indians at Bosque Redondo

1864—Kit Carson defeats the Navajo and Mescalero Apache Indians and forces them onto reservations

1876-1881—During the "Lincoln County War," two groups of settlers battle in New Mexico

1878—First railroad begins operating in New Mexico

1886—The Apache chief Geronimo surrenders

1888—New Mexico State University is founded

1889—University of New Mexico is founded

1900—Population of New Mexico is over 195,000

1912—On January 6, New Mexico becomes our 47th state

1916—Mexican Revolutionary General, Pancho Villa, raids Columbus, New Mexico

1917-1918—After the United States enters World War I, New Mexico provides over 17,000 men for the war effort

1922—Oil is found in New Mexico

1930—Carlsbad Caverns National Park is established

1941-1945—After the United States enters World War II, about 73,000 New Mexico men and women are in uniform. The famous 200th Coast Artillery Battalion, manned largely by New Mexico Hispanics, serves in the Philippines

1945—The world's first atomic bomb is exploded at New Mexico's Trinity Site

1950—A Navajo Indian, Paddy Martinez, discovers uranium in New Mexico

1955—Oil and gas discoveries are made in the Farmington area

1960—Santa Fe celebrates its 350th birthday

1962—Navajo Dam, located on the San Juan River, is dedicated

1964—The San Juan-Chama project, designed to bring water to the Albuquerque area, is begun

1969—N. Scott Momaday's, House made of Dawn, wins Pulitzer Prize for Literature

1972—Astronaut Harrison Schmitt, born in Santa Rita, explores the moon

1975—Jerry Apodoca is the first Hispanic governor elected since statehood.

1978—Bruce King is elected governor of New Mexico. Double Eagle II leaves Albuquerque and is the first balloon to successfully cross the Atlantic Ocean

1980—The Very Large Array of radio telescopes is dedicated near Socorro; they collect radio waves from far out in space

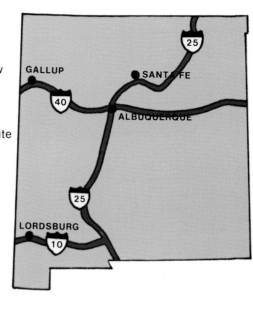

INDEX

adobe, 20, 23
agriculture, 15, 16, 38
Albuquerque, 20, 21, 42
Anasazi Indians, 5, 6
animals, 30, 31
Apache Indians, 13, 25, 26
Arizona, 11, 13, 19, 28
astronaut, 42
atom bomb, first, 17
atomic research, 17, 20
Aztec Ruins National Monument, 24
Bandelier National Monument, 24
Basketmakers, 5
bats, 35
Becknell, William, 10
Billy the Kid, 12, 39, 40
bird, state, 30, 44
blacks, 5
Bonney, William H. ("Billy the Kid"), 12, 39, 40
cactus plants, 32
Cactus State, 14
capital, state, 14, 22
Capitol, State, 22

Carlsbad Caverns National Park, 34, 35
cattle, 14, 17, 37, 38, 39
"Cattle Capital of the Southwest," 38
caves, 34, 35
Chaco Canyon National Monument, 24
Chavez, Dennis, 40
Chisum, John, 39
churches, 20, 23
Church of San Felipe de Neri, 20
cities (map), 47
Civil War, 12
Cliff Dwellers, 5
cliff dwellings, 5, 24
Clovis, 38
coal, 29
Colorado, 11, 19, 28
copper, 14, 15, 36
Coronado, 7, 15
cowboys, 37
crops, 16, 38, 38 (map)
Cuervo y Valdes, Francisco, 20
dams, 16

deserts, 31, 32
dinosaurs, 4
El Camino Real (The Royal Road), 7 (map)
El Rito, 28
Espanola, 28
Espejo, Antonio de, 8
ethnic groups, 20
explorers, 7, 8
farming, 15, 16, 38
Farmington, 29
flag, state, 44
flower, state, 32, 44
Folsom (town), 5
Folsom Man, 5
Folsom points, 5
forest, 30
fossils, 4, 5
Four Corners Monument, 28
fur trade, 10
Garrett, Elizabeth, 40
Garrett, Pat, 40
Geronimo (Chief), 13
ghost towns, 33
Gila National Forest, 30
gold, 6, 7, 11, 15

INDEX, Cont'd

gypsum sand, 34
Hernandez, 28
highways (map), 47
Hilton, Conrad, 42
history of state, 3-17
House of Representatives, United States, 40
Indian Achievement Award, 41
Indianapolis 500 race, 42
Indians, 3, 5-7, 9, 11, 13, 20, 22, 24-27, 32, 35, 40, 41
Inscription Rock, 8
irrigation, 16, 38
Kingston, 33
Lake Valley, 33
Land of Enchantment, 14
Las Cruces, 32, 33
Lincoln County War, 12, 39, 40
Los Alamos, 17
Los Chavez, 40
Madrid, 33
manufacturing, 20
maps:
  cities, 47
  crops, 38
  El Camino Real (The Royal Road), 7
  highways, 47
  population, 45
  Santa Fe Trail, 10
  state symbols, 44
  transportation, 47
Marcos de Niza, 7
Martinez, Julian, 41
Martinez, Maria Montoya, 41
mastodons, 4
Mauldin, Bill, 42

McJunkin, George, 5
Mexican War, 11
Mexico, 6, 7, 10, 11, 19
minerals and mining, 3, 8, 11, 14, 15, 29, 35, 36
Mission of San Miguel, 23
missions, 9
Mogollon, 33
Mountain Park, 42
mountains, 19, 45 (map)
Museum of New Mexico, 23
museums, 20, 22, 23, 37
National Atomic Museum, 20
national forest, 30
national monuments, 24, 34
national park, 34, 35
natural gas, 15, 29, 35, 36
Navajo Indian Reservation, 25, 27
Navajo Indians, 25-27
Nevada, 11
New Mexico, derivation of name, 8
New Mexico State University, 32-33
nicknames, state, 14
nuclear energy, 17, 20, 36
Nuevo Mexico, 8
nut pine (piñon) trees, 30
oil, 15, 29, 35, 36
O'Keeffe, Georgia, 41
Oklahoma, 19
Old Town, Albuquerque, 20
Oñate, Juan de, 8
outlaws, 12, 39
Palace of the Governors, 22
Pecos River, 19

piñon (nut pine) trees, 30
plants, 32
Popé (Pueblo Indian), 9
populations, 3, 11, 14, 25, 45 (map)
potash, 36
priests, 9
Pueblo Indians, 6, 7, 9, 22, 25, 26, 41
pueblos, 6
Puye Cliff Dwellings, 24
railroads, 14
ranching, 15, 17, 37, 39
reservations, Indian, 25, 27
Rio Grande river, 19, 32
rivers, 19, 45 (map)
road, oldest in United States, 7
roadrunner, 30
Roswell, 37
Roswell Museum and Art Gallery, 37
Royal Road, The (El Camino Real), 7 (map)
ruins, Indian communities, 24
Sacramento Mountains, 19
San Antonio, 42
sand, gypsum, 34
Sangre de Cristo Mountains, 19
San Ildefonso Pueblo, 41
San Juan de Los Caballeros, 8
Santa Fe, 8, 10, 14, 22, 23
Santa Fe Trail, 10, 10 (map)
Santa Rita, 42
Schmitt, Harrison, 42
seal, state, 44
senators, United States, 40, 42
Seven Cities of Cibola, 6

sheep, 15, 17, 37
Ship Rock, 27
silver, 11
Silver City, 39
Smith, Van C., 37
Socorro, 28
songs, state, 40
Southwestern Indian Polytechnic Institute, 21
Spanish, 6-10, 11, 15, 22
Spanish Americans, 20, 28
spiders, 31
State Capitol, 22
statehood, 14
state symbols, 44
Sunshine State, 14
Taos, 41
Territory of New Mexico, 1
Texas, 19
transportation (map), 47
tree, state, 30, 44
trees, 30
Trinity Site, 17
University of Albuquerque
University of New Mexico,
Unser, Al, 42
uranium, 15, 36
Utah, 11, 19, 28
Velarde, 28
White, Jim, 35
White Sands Missile Rang
White Sands National Monument, 34
wilderness areas, 29
World War I, 17
World War II, 17, 42
yucca plants, 32
Zuni Mountains, 19

About the Author:

Dennis Fradin attended Northwestern University on a creative writing scholarship and graduated in 1967. While still at Northwestern, he published his first stories in *Ingenue* magazine and also won a prize in *Seventeen's* short story competition. A prolific writer, Dennis Fradin has been regularly publishing stories in such diverse places as *The Saturday Evening Post, Scholastic, National Humane Review, Midwest,* and *The Teaching Paper.* He has also scripted several educational films. Since 1970 he has taught second grade reading in a Chicago school—a rewarding job, which, the author says, "provides a captive audience on whom I test my children's stories." Married and the father of three children, Dennis Fradin spends his free time with his family or playing a myriad of sports and games with his childhood chums.

About the Artist:

Len Meents studied painting and drawing at Southern Illinois University and after graduation in 1969 he moved to Chicago. Mr. Meents works full time as a painter and illustrator. He and his wife and child currently make their home in LaGrange, Illinois.